Stanley
in old picture postcards volume 1

by
Ronald Hindhaugh

European Library – Zaltbommel/Netherlands

GB ISBN 90 288 4596 8 / CIP

© 1988 European Library – Zaltbommel/Netherlands

Fourth edition, 1994: reprint of the original edition of 1988.

INTRODUCTION

This book does not set out to be a detailed historical documentation of Stanley and its surrounding villages; what it hopes to do is provide a trip down memory lane for older readers, and for younger readers give some insight into what the district looked like from the turn of the century up until the early thirties.

The place to start must be Tanfield, this being one of the oldest parts of the district. This takes its name from the river Thame or Tame that runs through the village. Tanfield was first mentioned around 900 when a church was built by the monks of Chester-le-Street. In the early 11th century William the Conqueror noted the village as a manor. The church was then rebuilt on more spacious lines. In 1286 Bishop Bek founded a collegiate church in Chester-le-Street and Tanfield was given to the fifth prebend as a chapelry. Since then the manor and tithes have been held by various people including Bertram Montboucher in the 14th century and Thomas Harbottle in the 16th century.

The larger buildings in the village date back to the 17th and 18th century and some, such as Tanfield Hall, still stand today. Most of the old village no longer exists, new housing estates have been built and a small industrial estate stands just on the outskirts. However, the village still retains much of its rural charm.

A little to the south-east of Tanfield is Shield Row. The word 'shiel' means a shepherd's summer hut. Before coal mining became of primary importance in the district sheep rearing and wool production were the main sources of work, hence the need for the huts or 'shielings'.

Shield Row was well-known because of its mining activities long before the present town of Stanley came into being, the Hare Pit, Hound Pit and Knap Pit being some of the mines working in the area.

The village had its own brewery which supplied ale to the public house nearby. This public house is the setting for a Geordie dialect song by Tommy Armstrong (the pitman's poet) called 'The Cat Pie'. At the top of Shield Row bank is Stanley itself. Stanley can trace its history back to the Romans who used a roughly built cattle camp to supply their fort at Newcastle and South Shields. The site of this second and third century camp was confirmed by Sir Nicholas Tempest in 1730 when he found coins, swords and other artefacts in the area. The Romans also built a raised road or causeway from Stanley to South Shields, part of which is still followed by modern roads.

Stanley was a very small village until about 1832 when

the West Stanley Colliery was sunk. Other collieries were soon working and the village began to develop not only in size but also in importance. By the late 1870's at least four collieries were in operation. These were the West Stanley, Louisa, Kettle Drum and Fanny collieries. All these have now gone, the Louisa being the last one to close. The Louise Sports Centre which opened in 1980, stands opposite the site of this old colliery.

With such a large number of collieries working in the area mining disasters were not unknown. The worst of these occurred at the West Stanley, or as it was better known, the Burns Pit.

There are comparatively few old buildings in Stanley, most, including the churches, were built in the 19th and early 20th centuries. A by-pass has recently been constructed to take traffic away from the Front Street which has now been pedestrianized.

South Moor, like Stanley, was a mining village. The first colliery to be sunk was the West Craghead in 1840. This later became known as the William or Billy Pit. The village grew up around this colliery and continued growing as more coal was found. Sadly today there are no collieries working in South Moor.

Being a relatively 'new' village there are few old build-ings, the school and church are among the oldest. Most of the colliery houses were built at the turn of the century. Some of these have been demolished to allow modern old people's bungalows to be built. Other modern buildings include the library and a new Working Men's Social Club which opened in 1981.

Annfield Plane (the spelling changed to Plain around 1853), which lies to the west of Stanley, is first mentioned in the Lanchester Register of 1778-1796. A former mining village, it includes Catchgate and Hare Law along with other small villages. Again, most of the buildings are relatively recent, the older ones being mid-19th century.

On 1st October 1896 Annfield Plain Urban District was formed. It was made up from the parishes of Greencroft Within, Collierley, Pontop and Kyo. Then, in 1937, it merged with the former Stanley and Tanfield Urban Districts and the Craghead Parish to form the Stanley Urban District Council.

March 1974 saw this Urban District, which also included Tantobie, Dipton and Burnopfield, merge with Consett to become the new Derwentside District.

1. Tanfield National School, or as it was later to be known, the Board School, was opened in 1844. Mr. Robert Agar, the first master, lived in the school house for more than 56 years. In 1962 the school was demolished after standing empty for many years. Note the thatched roofed cottages on the right where Hawthorne Terrace now stands.

ST. MARGARET'S CHURCH, TANFIELD.

2. The first church at Tanfield was constructed around 900 by the monks of Chester-le-Street. It was later enlarged after the Norman Conquest. The church, which is dedicated to St. Margaret, was almost entirely rebuilt in 1749. It has been restored and improved several times since then. The tower was built in the mid-19th century, the clock being added in 1919 as a war memorial.

Tanfield Village.

3. Here we see the Pack Horse Inn (now the Sea Horse), which took its name from the time before stage coaches when goods had to be carried on the backs of horses. Next door to the inn which is about 250 years old, is the blacksmith shop.

4. A view of Tanfield in about 1920. This shows a few of the old streets that were demolished many years ago. On the left is Waggon Row, just beyond is the Pack Horse and Front Street, and in the distance is the Board School. Part of the housing estate, St. Margaret's Drive, was built on the site where Front Street once stood.

5. This is Tanfield Hall, once the old Manor House, which dates back to the 17th and 18th centuries. Tanfield Boarding Academy was housed in the hall from about 1763 until 1860. The gates – which are said to be among the best in County Durham – were made by the village blacksmith in about 1730. It wasn't until 1958 that these needed restoring and this was done at Shotley Bridge.

6. The Causey Arch was built in 1727 at a cost of £12,000. It was built for Colonel Liddell and the Honourable Charles Montague, by a local mason, Ralph Wood. He originally built an arch out of wood, but this collapsed. Mr. Wood is said to have killed himself for fear that the stone one would do the same. It still stands today and is claimed to be the oldest single span railway bridge in the world.

7. This postcard shows the author's grandfather, father and uncles, who for many years were choiristers in St. Margaret's Church.

Shield Row Station

8. Shield Row Station was opened around 1894 by its first station master, Mr. W.S. Newton. In its heyday it excelled all the other stations on the Annfield Plain branch line, and it was not unusual for it to take £100 before noon on Saturdays.

9. A view of Station Road from the top of Shield Row bank, wrongly captioned on the post-card as **Manor Road**. The houses shown here were built between 1902 and 1904.

Bank Top, Shield Row.

10. A different view of Shield Row bank circa 1910. The ornate lamps which adorn the top of the gate pillars are sadly no longer there.

West Shield Row

11. A postcard, postally used in 1911, showing a view looking toward Tanfield Lea. The houses in the foreground form part of Barn Hill, and Sunny Terrace is on the right. The collieries, which can just be seen, are the West Shield Row, Tanfield Lea and the Wind Pit. These ceased to operate many years ago and nothing now remains of these once productive pits.

The Poplars, Shield Row.

Shield Row Station.

Council Chambers

West Stanley.

Front Street.

New Town Hall.

12. A 'multi-view' postcard of Stanley showing a few places of interest, some of which will be featured later.

St. Andrew's Church, West Stanley. (994)

13. St. Andrew's, built in 1876 at a cost of £4,409, is the parish church of Stanley. Prior to this church being built people had to travel to Tanfield to worship.

Parish Church, Stanley. 1236

14. The foundation stone for the tower, at the west end of the church, was laid in June 1930. It was consecrated less than a year later in January 1931. Today the church also has a clock, but this was not set in motion until 1952.

15. An interior view of St. Andrew's. This shows the altar screen and pulpit.

16. This is Stanley's Theatre Royal which stood in Station Road. Opened in 1903, it had a relatively short life of 27 years as it was destroyed by a fire in 1930.

17. A football team made up from members of the Theatre Royal staff in 1926.

18. Mark H. Lindon was the first lessee and manager of the Victoria Theatre. He and his wife then formed the Stanley Theatre Company which built the Theatre Royal. Here we see him as the 'Wolf' in a production at the theatre, in which his wife played 'Starlight Bess'.

19. A later view of Station Road to the one shown previously. On the left we can see the Market Hall. The original 'Paddy's Market' (named after Ireland's Patron Saint) occupied various sites before moving to Station Road in 1924. Moving down the street we come to what was once the Victoria Working Men's Club.

Barnhill, Stanley.

20. This is Barn Hill in around 1920. Very little has changed since then.

21. Built circa 1860 by Mr. James Forster, 'Paddy Rock's', or to give it its real name, the Stanley Inn, was the first public house in Stanley. On a more personal note, the gentleman who sent this card can be seen standing on the extreme left.

22. This is how the old road to East Stanley looked in about 1910. St. Andrew's Church Institute is on the left and on the right is the old police station, its lamp just visible above the door. In the late 1960's and early 1970's the police station and most of the other buildings were demolished to make way for the town centre bypass.

POST OFFICE, STANLEY. (582)

23. The Post Office mentioned on the card was owned by Mr. M.G. Armstrong who became postmaster in 1902 when Mr. Mallams, the first postmaster, retired. The Royal Hotel which can also be seen was opened on 24th November 1898.

Front Street, Stanley.

24. This is 'Aynsley's Buildings' built in 1888 by, as the name suggests, Mr. Aynsley. The shops have been owned by various people including Fred Elliott, who's shop is seen here. The Victoria Theatre, on the right, was originally intended as a public house (it could not get a licence). It opened, on 29th June 1893, with an Irish farce called Muldoon's Picnic. Two years later the Victoria Working Men's Club was formed in the cellar. The old Vic theatre was demolished and in 1935 the Victoria Cinema – later to become the Esoldo – was opened.

WESLEYAN CHAPEL, WEST STANLEY.

25. The first Wesleyan Chapel was just across the street from the one shown in this card. The chapel shown here was built in 1899 and was noted for its beautiful accoustics. Sadly it was demolished in 1983.

OARD SCHOOLS FRONT ST. STANLEY.

26. Stanley Board or Central school stands on the site of a large garden. It was opened in 1891 and had a two storied extension added in 1899. The first headmaster was Mr. J.A. Hodgson. Walter Wilson's shop can also be seen and they still have a shop in Stanley.

Council Offices, Stanley. (985)

27. This impressive looking building houses the Council Offices which were opened in 1911.
Some readers will remember the shop next door as Roe's Café. This is now a Building Society.

FRONT ST. STANLEY

28. Archibald Ramsden's musical instrument shop opened on 18th May 1901. In 1881 Mr. Benjamin Riddle had opened Stanley's first printing business on the premises. Most of the buildings on this side of the street were built between 1880 and 1890.

Bird's Eye View of Stanley.

29. Taken before 1910 the photo shows Thorneyholme Terrace, and other streets too numerous to mention. Due to the redevelopment of Stanley most of these houses have now been replaced by modern shops and new roads.

30. Built between 1899 and 1902 St. Joseph and the Sacred Heart is the Roman Catholic church of Stanley. To make it more spacious it was enlarged and restored in 1909.

31. The Wesleyan Chapel at the bottom of the street has now been demolished but little else has changed since this photograph was taken in about 1910.

Front Street, Stanley. (990)

32. On the right of this card is Slater and Costelloe's shop. Some readers would have known this as 'Cossy's Pawnshop'. The building on the left is The Queen's Hotel, built in 1898, which stood on the site of 'Chaytor's Buildings'. One of the business premises in these buildings was let to Hodgkin, Barnett, Pease, Spence and Company, who were later to become Lloyd's Bank Limited.

33. The West Stanley Co-operative Society was formed in March 1876. The first store was on the opposite side of the street to the building shown here. It moved to this site in 1880 when a large general store was opened. Here we see the present building which was built in 1906. The large tower was used as a water tower to operate the sprinkler system in the store.

34. This is the road from Stanley to Annfield Plain. Louisa Terrace, on the right, was first built in 1867 but these houses were found to be too small, larger ones were built in 1894. The railway line formed part of a level crossing which was used until 1934.

35. The first full time Salvation Army band was formed at Consett in about 1880. It was not very long before other full time bands were formed, like this one at West Stanley.

In Loving Memory of
MARY DONNELLY,
DEARLY BELOVED DAUGHTER OF
THOMAS & MARY DONNELLY
OF STANLEY
WHO WAS CRUELLY PUT TO DEATH
DECEMBER 14TH 1908
AGED 10 YEARS

THIS MEMORIAL
WAS ERECTED BY
PUBLIC SUBSCRIPTION.

This Memorial was erected by the Public
of Stanley and District in Memory of,
"MARY DONNELLY,"
By Penny·Subscription, per J. Larkman.

36. This card ends the section on Stanley on a sad note with the story of Mary Donnelly. On 4th December 1908 Mary Donnelly, aged 10 years, disappeared. Her body was found later in a field behind the Pea Farm. One Jeramiah O'Conner was charged with her murder and committed for trial. He was found guilty and sentenced to death. His execution was carried out in February 1909, but it went almost unnoticed as this was the month of the Burns pit disaster.

Burns Colliery Where Accident Occurred
West Stanley

37. Two accidents had already occurred at the Burns Colliery before 1909. The first, in 1865, when two men were killed, the second in 1882, when 13 were killed, then, at 3.45 pm on Tuesday 16th February 1909, 168 (as many spots as there are on a set of dominoes) men and boys were to lose their lives in two terrific explosions.

OLLIERY DISASTER AT WEST STANLEY – SCENE AT THE PIT HEAD. 1.

38. Crowds started to gather at the pit head almost immediately, waiting to hear any news of the victims. Telegrams of sympathy from the King and Queen were read out. As night fell arc lights were set up and still the crowds waited. It was to be a week of waiting for the people of Stanley.

39. At first it was not known what had caused the explosion. It was many years later when an explanation was found, a so called 'safety lamp' was thought to have been to blame, although this was never proved.

40. This is Mark Henderson, who was a deputy in charge of the Tilley seam at the time of the disaster. He was trapped along with a group of men in a small air pocket. Leaving the safety of this air pocket to try and find help, he managed to get word to the surface that 26 men were still alive. The men were finally rescued after being trapped for 14 hours.

41. This is Billy Gardener and his pony 'Paddy' which he rescued from the pit. Billy and Paddy later took a pit tub around the streets collecting money for the victims' families. Paddy and six other ponies were the only ones to be brought out of the pit alive.

42. The funerals of the men started to take place on the following Sunday. The procession and burials were said to have been watched by at least 150,000 people.

The Trench
at Stanley

43. Most of the men were buried in big trenches at St. Andrew's graveyard. Another trench was dug at St. Joseph's for the Roman Catholics.

44. A few were buried in private graves, such as the one shown here of an 18 year old boy.

45. This is 'Benton', a steam engine at the Burns Pit. What its actual role was in the disaster is not known.

IN LOVING MEMORY OF
The 151 MINERS WHO LOST THEIR LIVES
In the WEST STANLEY PIT EXPLOSION,
WHICH OCCURRED ON TUESDAY, FEB. 16th, 1909.

And as an expression of sympathy for the bereaved families.

___

They left their homes in perfect health,
And little thought of death so nigh,
But God thought fit to take them home,
And with his will we must comply.

___

The King says—
" He is terribly shocked and much grieved at the appalling colliery disaster which has occurred in your district, and at the fearful loss of life which it has entailed."

The Queen says—
"She wishes to express her deepest sympathy with the poor widows and families who have lost their nearest and dearest in this terrible colliery disaster."

46. One of the many 'in memory' cards sold at the time to aid the families of the men who lost their lives.

47. This card shows a view of South Moor in the early 1930's. The William or Billy Pit, sunk around 1840, was the heart of this community.

48. Built between 1897 and 1898, St. George's has been the parish church of South Moor since 1912.

49. South Moor's first Primitive Methodist Church was built in 1894. With the ever growing popularity of methodism it was found necessary to build a larger church. In April 1900 the opening ceremony took place at the church shown in this picture.

50. South Moor park was opened on 10th July 1920. It was originally a memorial to the employees of South Moor Colliery Company who died in the First World War. Their names are inscribed on two stone tablets on either side of the gates. Two smaller tablets have since been added to commemorate the residents of South Moor who lost their lives in the Second World War.

Memorial Park, South Moor 5046

51. The tennis courts, which are still very much in use, are just visible on the left. A pavillion now stands in front of the bowling green. The railway line, which can be seen in the distance, ran from the Headley Pit to the Louisa Pit at Stanley.

Memorial Park, South Moor, 12306

52. The band stand in the park is now in ruins and can no longer be seen. Trees and bushes cover the spot.

53. The Miner's Hall was opened in 1898. It had a library with a reading room and also a games room. The hall was used for dances and concerts and also for variety shows. In 1901 the first animated picture show to be seen in South Moor was given in this hall by a Mr. Carlyon.

54. The first colliery offices were in the colliery grounds. They were closed in 1906 when these offices were built. The manager's house 'The Limes', was incorporated into the building and was the first house in South Moor to have a bathroom.

55. The South Moor branch of the West Stanley Co-op was opened on 18th August 1900. The main branch at Stanley was closed for the day and a procession of the co-op horses and vehicles took place. Tea was given in a marquee at the store fields. Later that night a concert was held in the co-op hall at Stanley.

MAIN STREET, SOUTH MOOR (895)

56. The houses and shops seen here were all built at the turn of the century. Matthew Martin, Walter Wilson and Mr. Bambridge all had shops in this street.

57. Tommy's Lane or lonnon was named after Tommy Daglish who had the sole rights to gather horse manure from this lane. Tommy's arch, which stood at the top of this hill, was named after the same man.

BOARD SCHOOLS, SOUTH MOOR.

58. The Board School, or, as it is known today, Greenland School, was built in 1908. It takes its name from Greenland Villas which stood nearby.

59. A picture of one of the other schools in South Moor. Nu doubt readers will have fond, or perhaps not so fond, memories of it.

Craghead & South Moor Hospital   9632

60. The Holmside and South Moor miners welfare hospital, to give it its correct name, was opened in February 1927. Before this hospital was built injured miners had to be taken to the Royal Victoria Infirmary at Newcastle.

61. Front Street Craghead as it was circa 1915. Some of the business premises in the early days were owned by Tom Armstrong the general dealer, Mr. Marsh the postmaster and Mr. Wilson who was the cobbler.

Front Street, Craghead. 5712

62. Little has changed since this photograph was taken in the 1920's. One notable building on the left is the John and Castle Inn. Opposite is a three storied building owned at one time by Mr. C. Buckton who had a drapery, hairdressing and billiards business.

63. A Craghead United footballer from the 1910-11 season. The team was in fact a very good amateur side, winning the Durham amateur cup three times in succession 1910, 1911 and 1912.

64. The Ox Inn seen here was formerly known as the Bull Inn, a one-storied building which stood in front of the present one. This was demolished when the Ox was built. A well-known sportsman in the area, Mr. John Errington, was the landlord of the Ox Inn from 1863 to 1907. During this time he organised many sporting events in the fields behind the inn.

65. Like all miners halls at the time, New Kyo miners' hall had games rooms and a dance hall. Unlike the other halls it had a doctor's surgery. About a year after it was built (1912), a fire partially destroyed the building. Due to this, Doctor Parry, who had the surgery, lost all his surgical instruments and equipment. The building was later rebuilt.

66. Sunk in 1869, the Morrison Colliery was one of a number in the area. A little to the South East of this two other shafts were sunk in 1924, which were to be known as the Morrison Busty Colliery. Production ceased altogether in 1973.

67. This card shows Durham Road as it was in about 1911. The means of transport and the road conditions have changed considerably since then. Trains no longer use the bridge in the background but it still stands today.

68. Front Street Annfield Plain circa 1910. The ornate circular structure in the foreground used to be an underground toilet. These were demolished in 1917. Note the steam engine standing at the crossings. These crossings were part of the Stanhope and Tyne railway. They were dismantled in 1959.

69. A view of West Road Annfield Plain, again about 1910, showing the road to Stanley. Much of this has now changed. One of the buildings, the co-op, has been dismantled brick by brick and rebuilt at Beamish Open Air Museum. H. Nicklas, pork butcher and Hunters, the names on the awnings, will bring back memories to some people.

70. Greencroft Hall was built by the Clavering family in 1670. They lived in this beautiful building for over two hunderd years until 1880 when it was passed on to a French relative. The last owner of the estate, shipowner Robert Eales, moved out in about 1932. It was then used by the army during the Second World War. When the army moved out it sadly fell into disrepair and had to be demolished.

GREENCROFT HALL TOWERS, LANCHESTER   (655)

71. This ornate castellated arch was Greencroft Towers. It was for a long time the main roadway into the Hall. The whole estate was affected by mining subsidence and in 1955 the tower was condemned and then demolished.

FREE LIBRARY. & U. M CHURCH CATCHGATE

72. In 1908 Mr. Andrew Carnegie generously donated £3,000 to enable Annfield Plain Council to build the library shown here on the left. It is now scheduled as an historical monument. The United Methodist Chapel, on the right, had its foundation stone laid on 2nd July 1902 and opened officially in June 1903.

CATCHGATE & CHURCH. (915)

73. A view looking toward Harelaw perhaps about 1910. The church shown on the card, built in 1840, is dedicated to St. Thomas. The first Vicar was the Reverend T. Jackson. At the foundation stone laying ceremony, three coins from the reign of Queen Victoria, were put into a bottle and placed into a cavity of stone.

DELIGHT PIT. DIPTON. 1215.

74. This is Drelight Colliery which was sunk in 1912 and closed in 1940. Coal had been mined around the Dipton area for a number of years before this pit was sunk. Boring operations for coal had started in Dipton as early as 1731.

Derwent View, Burnopfield. 4433

75. Very little has changed since this picture was taken in the early 1920's. A few houses have since been built to replace the ones shown on the right, but, all in all a very similar view would be seen today.

76. Busty Bank Mill, Burnopfield circa 1920. This was once a thriving business but unfortunately it was demolished many years ago.